The Gospel
OF THE
God
OF Existence

BY ALTHEMUS JOSEPH DELAHOUSSAYE III

The Gospel

of the

God

of Existence

BY ALTHEMUS JOSEPH DELAHOUSSAYE III

508 West 26th Street
KEARNEY, NE 68848
402-819-3224
info@medialiteraryexcellence.com

The Gospel of the God of Existence

ISBN (Paperback): 978-1-958082-64-5

ISBN (Ebook): 978-1-958082-65-2

Printed in the United States of America

FOREWORD

This book doesn't even be anything other than a kind of outline of certain things covered in the Table of Contents. Briefly stated, the book is trying to give a little glimpse of the purpose for which God revealed Himself through several human beings.

Truth to me isn't anything other than living a decent life. A little bit of Truth spread throughout your life doesn't even be anything other than a little light shining from your soul. Truth is the admonitions and the precepts and the commandments and other guidance given in the Holy Scriptures. When you obey these precepts, admonitions, commandments, and other guidance, you're wearing the angelic, saintly, divine, and godly garments that God made for you to wear. Little do you know it, but the armor of God is the virtues and the qualities and the attributes of the Creator. When you wear these things, in your demeanor and in your speaking about any little thing, the light of these qualities and attributes and virtues emanate from your soul and even affect other human beings, nothing other than saying, Truth isn't nothing other than many things. It's the way you carry yourself. The way that you carry yourself shows off the Truth that you believe in. When they say anything about certain people, it's a little fact that they sometimes say, "He carries himself like a king." Or they might say, "She carries herself like a queen." I don't know much about Truth, howbeit, the little truth of it is, I don't know little anything. I get my knowledge from the Scriptures. I don't understand anything about any little thing. Howbeit, when I read the Scriptures, I get a little understanding about what life is all about.

PROLOGUE

The reason why the God of Existence Created little human beings isn't any little reason. The Creator Created the Existences for the purpose of the human beings even some day traversing the Existences of the God of Existence. The Existences aren't even the same kind of Existences, nothing other than saying, meaning that every Existence is unique and even different from every other Existence. When the human being enters the so called heaven or paradise, he'll even be in a position to travel to other little planets. God the Creator didn't nothing other than Create the human beings to even enjoy traversing His Existences and even while traversing them, to grow and mature and develop and evolve into being more and more and more in the image and the likeness of the God of Existence. A little never ending journey of growing and maturing and developing and evolving more and more and more in the image and the likeness of their Creator.

TABLE OF CONTENTS

Chapter 1
Religion of the Creator

The religion of the Creator isn't anything other than revealed through a human being who's even chosen by the Creator. The chosen human being doesn't even have any choice in the matter. The chosen human being even revealed all of the religions of the Creator, meaning nothing other than, a chosen human being revealed each and every religion of the Creator, no little doubt whatsoever. The truth of the matter isn't nothing other than, the Creator **spoke through** the chosen human being. The religion of the Creator isn't even one religion as many human beings even be thinking. The Creator is infinitely diverse and even revealed all of the religions that are even currently known to humanity. When the Creator reveals His religions, He kind of hides the fact that He's the One speaking through a chosen representative. The Creator doesn't even like being identified as any little human being for the reason of it being, the Creator is even infinite in even every respect and not any little finite human being. That chosen human being isn't anything superior to any other human being. That chosen human being doesn't even be any special human being at all.

1

The Creator isn't even revealing any religion other than through a chosen human being. That chosen human being isn't nothing other than, even in some religions, having the same name as the Creator. The Gospels aren't nothing other than eye-witnessed accounts of what Jesus the Creator spoke through Jesus the human being. The Holy Quran isn't anything other than what the Creator revealed to the human being, Muhammad, through the Angel Gabriel. And even the Angel Gabriel wasn't anything other than God Himself as the Angel Gabriel. The Holy Quran calls the Creator nothing other than Allah, meaning nothing other than God in the English language. The chosen human being, Abraham, didn't even have any name for the Creator other than God, in his language. Moses knew the Creator as "I am that I am." Jesus the human being knew the Creator as the Father and even the Creator revealed Himself through the human being, Jesus, as the Son of the Living God. The human being Krishna didn't even be knowing the Creator by any name other than the Hindu name for the Supreme Being. The human being, Krishna, wasn't nothing other than even known as the Supreme Personality of the Godhead later on in the Hindu Scriptures, howbeit, **that** Krishna wasn't nothing other than the Creator manifesting Himself as

2

Krishna. The human being Buddha didn't even mention the Creator and only revealed the Creator through the technique of meditation, where even any meditator can discover that the Creator exists for his own self. The human being Zoroaster even revealed the Creator as Ahura Mazda, the God of Energy. The human being Mirza Hussein Ali didn't even mention the Creator as anything other than many little names that aren't anything other than attributes and qualities and virtues of the Creator, even only in inadequate little human language. The little human languages are even too inadequate to even describe anything infinitely Infinite.

When the God of Existence chooses His prophet, He endows His prophet with the station of even being more knowledgeable than other human beings. The prophet of the God of Existence isn't even any small little human being like the other human beings, nothing other than saying, the prophet of the God of Existence isn't anything other than more seeking His Creator than the other human beings. That little human being isn't any little prophet other than in the future when he or she acquires certain virtues and certain attributes and certain spiritual qualities. Little human beings that seek out their Creator in even every little thing were the little human beings chosen by the God of Existence to even be His

3

prophets, nothing other than saying, the former prophets weren't nothing other than seekers after their Creator. When little other human beings come to be seeking out their Creator also, they'll even be anointed with a little prophethood, no doubt whatsoever. When the little seekers after their Creator attain a little prophethood, they'll even attain a little godhood afterwards, no little doubt whatsoever. Little ignorant seeking human beings aren't nothing other than few and far between. Little ignorant seeking human beings after their Creator aren't even liking little unseeking little human beings for the reason of it being, seeking human beings live in their God. The little seeking human beings don't even like evil human beings other than to educate them as to their little purpose for being in the Existences of their Creator. Little seeking human beings don't even like educating close minded little human beings for the reason of it being, close minded little human beings don't even respond to the little educating words or exemplary actions of the little seeking human being. Little human beings don't even like hearing spiritual discourses for the reason of it being, they even dwell on trivial little information that they think is all too important. When the little ignorant trivial information isn't liked by the seeking human being, then the little ignorant pursuer of trivial information doesn't even like discoursing with the seeker of the God of Existence.

When little human beings seek out their Creator in even every little thing, they even see their Creator as the highest Thing that even Exists, nothing other than saying, little seekers of the God of Existence aren't any little thing like other little human beings. Seeking human beings aren't nothing other than in tune with Reality. Seeking human beings aren't any small little finite human beings at all.

Chapter 2
The Validity
of all of the Religions

The religions of the Creator aren't even anything other than kind of mentioned in Chapter 1, and, aren't nothing other than the major religions, howbeit, the Creator has even revealed numerous paths to Himself over the little millennia. The thought to be false polytheism isn't even any false religion at all. The Creator wasn't nothing other than all of the Gods of the polytheistic religions. The family of the major religions isn't anything other than the major belief systems of most of the human beings. That monotheistic belief isn't nothing other than the belief of most human beings today and isn't even anything other than the culminating belief of an evolving theism that has even been monitored and guided by the Creator into even finally evolving into a current belief held by most human beings. That human being isn't nothing other than the revealer of even the secular laws of the Creator, and even the revealer of technology that the Creator really reveals through human beings at the appropriate time for its revelation. The human being isn't anything other than, even every single one, guided in some way by the Creator to fulfil his little destiny. The Creator isn't even liking human beings to even suffer, howbeit, the suffering cleanses the soul and the consciousness of the human beings of their evil inclinations and even cleanses the soul and the consciousness of their attachment to trivial little material pursuits and little trivial material pleasures and even any little trivial thing.

When the little human beings begin to even seek out their Creator in even every little thing, then their Creator will even assist them to find their Creator even in their little consciousness. Little ignorant human beings don't even like being admonished, howbeit, the Creator admonishes the little ignorant human beings nothing other than to seek out their Creator.

Chapter 3
The prophets of the Creator

The Creator isn't nothing other than the Prophets, and, the vehicle through which the Creator speaks and does some little things that are even the things that the Creator wants done a little absolutely, aren't nothing other than the prophets of the Creator. God the Creator is the Prophet with a capital "P", and, the chosen human being is the prophet with a little lower case "p". When the Creator chooses to manifest Himself, he anoints His chosen vehicle with a human being prophethood. The Creator doesn't even be anything other than Jesus the Son of the Living God and even Jesus the human being isn't anything other than the chosen prophet of the Creator, whom God used to speak His Word to the human beings of a little two thousand little years ago or so. Jesus the Creator came to the human beings in the Station of "The Son of the Living God." That Jesus the prophet wasn't nothing other than hearing God speak to the other human beings even at the same time that the other human beings heard God speaking to them. God the Creator spoke to Jesus the human being even with only Jesus the human being hearing Him many little times, and, even Jesus the human being knew more about the Father than the other human beings. Jesus the Creator didn't even be liking Jesus the human being telling even anyone too much about what he heard only himself, for the reason of it being, Jesus the human being didn't fully understand everything that the Creator was even revealing to him. Jesus the human being didn't even like the cross that he was even nailed to, and, he even, on the cross, asked the Creator nothing other than, "Father, why hast Thou forsaken me?" The Creator didn't even not answer Jesus and even told Jesus the prophet nothing other than, "I haven't forsaken Jesus, howbeit, I'm letting Jesus know that the cross isn't even hurting Jesus as Jesus can even know for himself. Jesus isn't anything other than going to die in a few little minutes and even in three little days I will raise Jesus from the deceased condition that he's even in at that little time, and, I'll even let Jesus roam the countryside shocking many of My disciples, and, even in the little end I'll even cause your consciousness to ascend into My seventh heaven and even after that I'll even cause Jesus to even travel to India and even teach My Word to certain people of the Indian continent."

Jesus the Creator even spoke through Buddha, spoke through Krishna, spoke through Abraham, spoke through Moses, spoke through

Muhammad, and even spoke through Zoroaster, and even spoke through certain human beings that are unknown to most of humanity.

Little human beings that are chosen to be the prophets of the Creator aren't anything other than decent little human beings. When little ignorant human beings verbally criticize any prophet of their Creator, they're even really criticizing their Creator. Little ignorant human beings don't even really like what the prophets of the God of Existence readily say to them about certain little abstruse little things. When little ignorant human beings don't even like what is being said to them, they coil up like a little rattle snake ready to inject their venom into the prophet of righteousness.

Chapter 4
The Validity of all of the prophets

All of the major prophets are the intermediary that the Creator uses to communicate His Will to other human beings. The prophets aren't nothing other than chosen by the Creator as the vehicle of choice to communicate His Message and His Will to the other human beings. That prophet, Jesus the Buddha didn't even teach anything other than meditation, for the reason of it being, meditation causes the human consciousness to even be constantly kind of decent without any flagrant evil thoughts, for the most part. Abraham taught the human beings nothing other than, that there was only one God. Krishna taught the human beings nothing other than, God isn't any little thing but a little too complex for human beings to even comprehend even a little bit. Moses taught the human beings nothing other than, repeated that there was only one God, and even taught the Ten Commandments. Jesus taught human beings nothing other than, God was the Father of human beings, and that the human beings need to even do the Will of their Father. Muhammad taught the human beings nothing other than that the prophets were all from the

Creator and even revealed little stories telling the human beings about what happens to decent human beings and what happens to evil little human beings. Zoroaster taught the human beings nothing other than, God is all Power.

Chapter 5
The Unity of all of the Religions

All of the religions are unified, even unified in the sense of making the human beings try to even be as decent as they can even be. That human being doesn't even like always doing the decent little thing and even the soul of the human beings doesn't nothing other than cause the human beings to even feel ashamed or suffer a little lot of the times when they even do something evil. The Creator even monitors all the human beings for their decency and even causes most flagrant violators of His Will to even be caught and incarcerated or even taken care of in any way that the Creator deems suitable for their flagrant violations. The Creator even causes many sinners to even be transformed in their souls and their consciousness, and even in their forms for even upgrading their souls and their consciousness and their forms, for certain destinies of certain human beings to even be fulfilled at the appropriate little time.

All of the religions come from the Creator, no little doubt whatsoever.

When the religions don't agree with each other, it's because the God of Existence chose to create differences in the religions for the reason of causing the sincere adherents of the different religions to even accept whatever God revealed to other religions, no matter what it was. If all of the religions were the same, there would only be one religion and no diversity of religion. God the Creator doesn't want only one religion for the reason of it being, nothing other than, if all people were of the same religion, there wouldn't even be many little diverse thoughts on many little subjects. Little adherents of one world religion aren't anything other than very misguided for the reason of it being, one world religion would even make most little people think the same about even most little subjects. That wouldn't be conducive to the expansion of the consciousnesses of both little parties. When there are differences of opinion, the discussing parties need to think while expanding their consciousnesses into different and newer ways of thinking. When the thoughtful person thinks about a different point of view, he needs to even think in a newer little way to even understand the different point of view. When two people argue in a decent little argument, they need to start thinking a little differently in order to comprehend the point of view of the other person, and that's decent for growth and development and expansion and maturing and evolution of the minds of both of the discussing parties.

Chapter 6
The Oneness of the Creator

The Creator isn't nothing other than the only Creator that there even is. The polytheistic religions aren't even false religions. In the polytheistic religions, the One Creator is even all of the Gods in that polytheistic religion. The human beings even think that the ancient religions aren't nothing other than little false religions, howbeit, the ancient religions aren't nothing other than appropriate for the level of understanding of human beings at the time of their Revelation. Only the One True God is knowing that all of the religions aren't anything other than revealed by Him and Him Alone through His human being prophets. The One True God doesn't even be anything other than, in the Christian Religion nothing other than, the Father and even the Son and even the Holy Spirit. The human beings aren't anything other than living in the existences of the Highest Being That Exists, Who isn't nothing other than the Creator of Existence even in a newest Station of even being the Highest Being That Exists And Doesn't Exist And Is And Isn't, nothing other than saying, a newest God kind of means that even the Creation is even being

16

Recreated by the Creator. The former Creation isn't anything other than abrogated and a new Creation is coming into being in its stead. That old Creation didn't even be anything other than decent as can be, and, even in the newest Creation, the human beings will even be more thoroughly assisted in climbing the little ladder of progress for even attaining the first prophethood that'll even make the human beings even more prospering in the existences of the Highest Being That Exists And Doesn't Exist And Is And Isn't. That newest Creator won't even not help even the little evil human beings get to a newest condition of decency where they'll even attain that first human being prophethood also. The newest Creator isn't even nothing other than the Old Creator also, meaning nothing other than, the newest Creator isn't nothing other than just Ruling over His Voluminous Existences even in a newest Station that's even Infinitely, Infinitely, Infinitely, with infinite Infinitelys, Infinitely, Infinitely more Infinitely complex than the previous old Station. That human being prophethood of the human beings isn't nothing other than the first human being prophethood of unending higher prophethoods that the human beings will even attain to, nothing other than saying, the human being won't even be anything other than attaining many stations during his journey toward never ending forevermore. That human being isn't even as little as human beings even think human beings are. When that Creator created human beings, He created a soul that is even infinite in its little everything, and, it's even in a finite little space. The godhood of human beings isn't nothing other than attainable only after the first prophethood has even been attained, and, it's even only a station of a super-human human being, meaning nothing other than, a little super-human only in intelligence and feelings and qualities and attributes and virtues. That human being needs to even be very, very, very decent before the Creator gives him that human being godhood station. That godhood station doesn't even be anything other than a gift of the newest Creator to His creatures. That human being isn't even any creator potentially or in reality, howbeit, he's a helping creator of his own future selves even at higher and higher levels of the prophethood and the godhood stations. That godhood station doesn't even be nothing other than given only to the very, very, very decent human beings. The godhood stations aren't even having any ending and even the prophethood stations don't even be having any ending either. The newest Creator isn't nothing other than giving esoteric knowledge to the human beings when they even attain the prophethood station. And that godhood station even gives higher esoteric knowledge than the prophethood station.

When the little human beings limit their Creator, they're even very ignorant that the Creator is capable of doing even anything any human being can even conceive of. The Creator can even do anything that He can even conceive of, and no human being can even conceive of what the Creator can conceive of. When the human being limits his Creator by saying that the Creator won't do this or that or can't do this or that, the little human being is in grievous error, for the reason of it being, no human being can predict what the Creator will or won't do or even know what the Creator can or can't do.

Misinterpretation of Scripture even causes some little human beings to limit their Creator, howbeit, nothing other than saying, always, the Creator doeth Whatsoever He Willeth or Chooseth to Do!!!

Chapter 7
The Oneness of the Races

The races aren't anything other than one race. God made differences between the so called races for the reason of causing the human beings to even, of their own free will, determine that there is really only one race. When prejudice invades the human consciousness, even any kind of prejudice, it causes the soul of the prejudiced one to even be very close minded and even very blind to even esoteric knowledge that needs an open minded human being to understand it. Little do you know it, but, the so called races aren't even anything other than like the different flowers in a beautiful flower garden.

Little do you know it, but all things are living. An atom is a human being, and, a plant is a human being, and, an animal is a human being. They're all with a different little consciousness or what we call a different little mind set. When the atom isn't just inanimate matter, it's even just conscious of existing, and that is all!!! A little plant is conscious of existing and growing physically. An animal is conscious of existing and growing and developing and maturing and evolving even physically and a little mentally and emotionally and even a little spiritually. A so called two-legged human being is conscious of existing, is conscious of growing and developing and maturing and evolving spiritually and emotionally and physically and even mentally. The little two-legged human being even starts out in Existence as a little atom, and then enters the little plant kingdom, and then enters the little animal kingdom, and finally enters the little two-legged little human kingdom. Little ignorant two-legged little human beings aren't even liking what we're saying even now, nothing other than saying, after entering the little two-legged little human kingdom, the human being even needs to acquire certain attributes and certain spiritual qualities and certain spiritual virtues in order to prosper when he enters the next existence of the existences of the larger Existence of the God of Existence. When little human beings even die, they'll be Counseled about their lacking certain qualities and virtues and attributes and even enter heaven or paradise on the condition of them working hard to acquire the requisite characteristics needed to progress in the next existence, heaven or paradise.

Little birds aren't even little animals at all, they're little evolving human beings. Don't think that a little rattlesnake isn't a human being!!! It's a little evil human being that'll never enter the little two-legged human being kingdom. It'll reincarnate into the reptile kingdom even forevermore. The little human beings that are insects will even similarly always reincarnate into the little insect kingdom. The little other so called insects also will reincarnate back into the little insect kingdom. Even the little birds will always reincarnate back into the little bird kingdom. Only mammals reincarnate into the little two-legged little human kingdom. And then, only the most docile ones will even reincarnate into the little two-legged little human being kingdom. The ferocious animals in the mammalian class will always reincarnate as a ferocious animal only.

When the Creator created Existence, even before creating Existence, He knew what little souls would be evil and which little souls would even eventually be decent. The Creator didn't put any soul into Existence that would be so evil as to continually disrupt Existence. These only exist as a Memory in the Consciousness of the Creator. The little atoms aren't as evil as these souls, and, most little atoms will always be a little atom, even forevermore. Little plants aren't as evil as the permanent little atoms, that is, the permanent little plants that'll always be little plants even forevermore. The little animals aren't as evil as the little plants, that is, the permanent animals. The little two-legged little human beings are the most decent of the total human being population. Nothing other than saying, the seemingly evil ones aren't anything other than capable of being rehabilitated, eventually, with the assistance of their Creator.

The little ignorant evil human beings that aren't living at a decent little level, aren't anything other than hurting their little selves by not changing their little behavior into very decent behavior.

Little ignorant human beings that don't seek out their Creator will even be permanent little two-legged little human beings even for the rest of little never ending forevermore. When little human beings seek out their Creator, they even are anointed with a little prophethood. When the little prophet attains a satisfactory knowledge of Existence, he'll even be anointed with a little godhood little station. Little ignorant human beings who don't seek out their Creator will even be nothing other than little permanent human beings.

Chapter 8
The Validity
of the minor prophets

The minor prophets aren't nothing other than the human being prophets under the aegis of one of the Major Prophets. Moses was a major prophet who wasn't nothing other than the human being major prophet that the Creator, the Real Major Prophet, used to convey His Message to other human beings. All of the minor prophets and the major prophets aren't anything other than really all minor prophets. They're minor in the sense of the Creator always being the Major Prophet through a human being intermediary.

Nothing other than saying, the major prophets who were under the aegis of a Major Prophet, the God of Existence, aren't nothing other than Abraham, Moses, Jesus the Nazarene, Muhammad, Buddha, Krishna, and Zoroaster, who're the major ones known to most of humanity. When the major prophets aren't in the world, a minor prophet takes their place who is also under the aegis of the major prophet and even under the aegis of the One Major Prophet, the God of Existence. This meaneth nothing other than, the God of Existence is the Real Prophet and the little human being major and minor prophets are the human being form that the Creator uses to convey His Message to all the other human beings. Nothing other than saying, several minor prophets have come into this world. The twelve Imams of Shiite Islam were minor prophets under the aegis of Muhammad and the God of Existence. Joseph Smith wasn't nothing other than a minor prophet under the aegis of Jesus the Nazarene and the True Prophet, the God of Existence. The other minor prophets ae relatively unknown to most human beings and won't even be mentioned here. The God of Existence speaks through the major and minor prophets. The God of Existence hammers his Will into the major and the minor prophets for the reason of it being, they know more about the purpose of Existence and even more about the God of Existence than even any other human being.

Chapter 9
The Unity of the Creator

The Creator isn't nothing other than One Creator and only One. There aren't any three Creators or four or any number other than One. The Creator is united in every little thing. He is seen in literally everything, meaning some quality or some attribute or some virtue of the Creator is seen in everything that exists. In the stars, see the glory and magnificence of the Creator. In an atom, see the marvelous complexity of the Creator. In the Universe, see the power and awesome might of the Creator. In the human being see the intelligence of the Creator reflected in the intelligence of a little human being. And, in everything that exists there is a sign of the Creator. Little human beings aren't anything other than small compared to the Creator of little human beings and really, in comparison, little human beings don't even exist, comparatively speaking. The little human beings need to seek out their Creator in even every little thing, nothing other than saying, the little human beings are created to even search for their Creator, even in their consciousness. The Buddhist meditation isn't anything other than leading to the knowledge of the Creator; no doubt about it.

The Creator isn't nothing other than every human being, not even when they're evil. When the little human beings are evil, they're expressing their little free will. The Creator isn't any little thing that little human beings even think He is. The destiny of little human beings isn't nothing other than to be a creator. The little human beings aren't nothing other than doing the Will of their Creator. The little human beings aren't nothing other than controlled by their Creator for the most little part, howbeit, under certain situations the Creator allows the little human beings to do their own little will, and, even the Creator allowing a human being to do any little thing of his own free will, isn't anything other than exercising His Permissive Will. Nothing other than saying, every little thing that happens in Existence is the Will of the Creator, either by His Persuasive Will or His Permissive Will, and no little human being can thwart the Persuasive Will of the Creator.

When the little human beings mature and grow and develop and evolve even enough, then the Creator will control them completely and even then the little ignorant little human beings will even be the Creator as little ignorant human beings. The Creator guides even every little human being by His Persuasive Will into fulfilling their destiny.

That little Creator isn't little like many little ignorant human beings even believe the Creator is little. When the time is right, the Creator will supervise even every little human being in the art of creating their little human being selves and even supervise them for the rest of little never ending forevermore into even being higher and higher gods and higher and higher creators of their own selves and even highest little supreme beings that little human words are even incapable of even describing. The little human being, in his soul, has the potential to even be a being that can't even be described in little ignorant human vocabulary. When the little human being even surrenders his will to the Creator, he starts his little journey up Jacob's little ladder even at the highest rate of ascending Jacob's little ladder. When a human being grows and develops and matures and evolves, he doesn't even not become bored at his present little level, therefore, at the highest levels of progress, becoming a creator of his own little self is even necessary for the little human being. Even forevermore will little human beings tire of their present little level and even **always** be able to progress to a higher level.

When the little human being contemplates any little thing, he sees the Creator even in every little thing. Contemplate the little

Universe and you 'll even see the Creator as All-Powerful and Almighty. You'll even see Him as the Most Orderly Thing that even Exists. Contemplate even a little cave and you'll see the Creator as very Mysterious. Contemplate the Universe and even see the Creator as more than your little understanding can even fathom. Contemplate your own little self and see the Creator standing within your little soul, Mighty and Powerful and Self-Subsisting. That little Creator even isn't little or as big as a few little human beings even believe that He is. Those who believe that the Creator is bigger than even Existence or even Infinity aren't nothing other than a little deluded by their inadequate comprehension of how big the Creator really is. The Creator surrounds Infinity, surrounds the surrounding of Infinity and even surrounds any surrounding even for the infinite little level of surrounding little Infinity. There is no end to the Infiniteness of the Creator. How big is Infinite??? The Creator is Infinite in even every Quality and every Attribute and every Virtue and even Infinite in everything about the Creator. That Creator can even Will even anything any little human being can even conceive of, and, even Will anything He can even conceive of, and, no little human being can even conceive of what the Creator can conceive of!!!

The Creator can even be a little human being and even mingle with little ignorant human beings, and, He can even let little ignorant human beings be a little bigger than He is, and even whip the hell out of the bigger little human being who even thinks the Creator is smaller than he is and subject to his little authority. God the Creator can even make any little human being into whatever God wants that little human being to even be!!! With that I'll end the little discussion!!!

Chapter 10
Purpose of Living in Existence

The purpose of living in the existences of the Creator isn't nothing other than to acquire virtues and attributes and spiritual qualities. When the little human being is born, he's devoid of any knowledge at all and needs to learn everything about how to care for himself and even acquire virtue and attributes and spiritual qualities to even prepare himself for entry into the next existence of the Creator which is known as heaven or paradise. When the human being doesn't acquire the necessary virtue and attributes and spiritual qualities for advancing to heaven or paradise, the little human being will be Counseled by the God of Existence after his little demise and even allowed to enter heaven or paradise on the condition of him or her working to acquire more spiritual characteristics necessary for progress in the heaven or paradise of the God of Existence.

When a little human being is prejudiced racially or religiously or any other way, he's a little ignorant that the heaven or paradise existence is a little non-religious denomination existence and a multi-racial existence. Why would the Creator allow a prejudiced human being to enter His heaven or His paradise??? Even eliminating little evil prejudices isn't anything other than necessary along with acquiring spiritual virtue and spiritual qualities and spiritual attributes in preparation for entering the heaven or paradise of the Creator!!! When a little human being is prejudiced against any little thing, he's close minded and even a little narrow minded human being that needs to open his little mind so that the Creator can fill it with decent knowledge. When the little human being continues his little evil prejudices, the Creator will undoubtedly Counsel that little human being at his little demise.

The purpose of being in the existences of the Creator isn't anything other than for the little ignorant human beings to grow and mature and develop and evolve into being more in the image and the likeness of their Creator even forevermore. Nothing other than saying, little ignorant human beings believe many little things, howbeit, they **know** very little about Existence. When the little ignorant human beings enable their little selves to grow and mature and develop and evolve into being more in the image and the likeness of their Creator, then they'll even begin to learn about Existence and even start **knowing** certain little things instead of believing certain little things!!!

Little ignorant human beings aren't realizing that the epitome of knowledge for a little ignorant human being isn't anything other than to realize "The human being **knows** nothing." Little human beings only believe in certain little things!!! Beliefs aren't anything other than a little lowest understanding of a higher knowledge. All little beliefs of human beings aren't anything other than eventually going to be supplanted by a little knowledge of the little subject about which little human beings have some belief. Religious truths aren't anything other than beliefs that are the lowest understanding of a higher knowledge that we'll even call "Truth." The little scientific truths are even the little lowest understanding of a higher knowledge also.

Chapter 11
Why the Reincarnation

While in the atom existence and the plant existence and even in the so called animal existence, little human beings are reincarnated until they are sufficiently developed and evolved to enter the little two-legged little human being little kingdom.

Why would the Creator allow an immature human being devoid of spiritual qualities and spiritual attributes and virtue to enter his heaven or paradise??? Nothing other than saying, spiritual qualities and spiritual attributes and spiritual virtue are necessary for maturing and any human beings who don't grow and develop and mature and evolve while in this existence aren't anything other than depriving themselves of the purpose for which they were even created.

When a little human being is lacking spiritual qualities and spiritual virtue and spiritual attributes at the appointed little hour of his little demise, the Creator will even Counsel that little human being, no little doubt, and even allow that little human being to enter heaven with the little condition of that little human being changing his little ignorant little behavior and working to acquire the needed spiritual characteristics needed for progress in the heaven or paradise of the God of Existence.

Chapter 12
What is the Ultimate Purpose of Existence

The ultimate purpose of Existence is for the human being to live happily in the existences of his Creator even ever growing and developing and maturing and evolving to even become more in the image and the likeness of his Creator, even forevermore.

The purpose of Existence isn't anything other than providing a milieu suitable for the little ignorant human being to grow and develop and mature and evolve in many little qualities and many little virtues and many little attributes, even in knowledge and even in growing in the little emotions. Many little ignorant human beings aren't growing and developing and maturing and evolving of their own free will simply because of their ignorance of their purpose for being in the Existence of their Creator. The ultimate purpose of Existence isn't one little thing. It's very multi-faceted. When the little ignorant human beings begin to fulfill their purpose in the Existence, they'll even become happier and even more confident in even everything that they even undertake to accomplish. When the little ignorant human being attains even a little knowledge about Existence, he'll even be very powerful in his consciousness. Knowledge, real knowledge, expands the consciousness. Little information that's prevalent in society today doesn't expand the consciousness one little bit. Knowledge is the knowing of the underlying reality of something, rather than just superficial qualities which is what the current information is that pervades the current little society. When the little human being learns to attain the most decent character, the Lord of Existence will even reveal some knowledge to him or her that'll even confound the little human being and even confer an expanded consciousness on that little individual. Knowledge is what the Creator is knowing about even every little thing that even exists. Information is what is prevalent in the little modern society. Knowledge can even cause society's little transformation. Knowledge of the purpose of life isn't nothing other than necessary to cause the happiness of the little ignorant human beings, nothing other than saying, knowledge of the purpose of life will even transform the entire world community into a very organized, fruitful, goal oriented world community.

MEDITATION: Meditation is a key to expanding the consciousness of little human beings. When the Buddhist people meditate, they close their eyes, sitting in a comfortable little position, and even start forcing out all little thoughts out of their consciousness. Little by little they start controlling the little extraneous thoughts and have a clear consciousness, without any distracting little thoughts.

After learning to control extraneous little thoughts, the meditator concentrates on his consciousness, and, even expands his consciousness just by concentrating on his clear little consciousness.

After learning to control little extraneous thoughts, the meditator can even concentrate on one little subject, and, new little thoughts about that little subject will even pop into his little consciousness.

Even after learning to control extraneous little thoughts, the meditator can even concentrate on one little word, and, thoughts about that little word will even pop into his little consciousness. For instance, if the meditator thinks about "love", thoughts about love will even pop into his little consciousness.

When the meditator learns to concentrate on concentrating, the meditator will even increase his ability to concentrate. The key is to focus on one little subject, or one little word, or one little thought, and concentrate as hard as possible on that little subject or that little word or that little thought, thereby strengthening the concentration ability of the little meditator.

When the meditator grows and develops and matures and evolves in character and thought and decent behavior, the Lord of Existence will even start speaking to him in his little consciousness. Then the little meditator strengthens his meditative and concentrating ability by listening to the Voices of the Lord of Existence. The little meditator will even grow and develop and mature and evolve in concentration and even be more aware of his surroundings at all little times. When the meditator learns to be as decent as he can be, the Lord of Existence will even grant him certain little consciousness powers that require very deep concentration ability, nothing other than saying, the power of a Guru lies in his concentration ability and that's all meditation trains the little human being to even be doing, is concentrating at the highest level possible!!!

So, expanding the consciousness is one of the purposes of being in the Existence of the Lord of Existence. For, when the consciousness is expanded, the Lord of Existence can grant that little consciousness powers that aren't nothing other than supernatural. Little by little every human being is a little consciousness expanding human being, for the reason of it being, life's little circumstances cause consciousness expansion even a little bit. The meditation practiced by the experienced meditator expands the consciousness more than any other thing, even life's little circumstances.

LEVELS OF CONSCIOUSNESS: There are seven levels of consciousness that most human beings are living their little lives in. A saintly human being sometimes acts on a godly or a divine or an angelic level of consciousness, and, sometimes acts on a spiritual or a human or an animalistic level of consciousness. Howbeit, a saintly human being mostly acts or thinks on a saintly level of consciousness.

The Seven Steps to Heaven up Jacob's Ladder

The Godly Level of Consciousness
The Divine Level of Consciousness
The Angelic Level of Consciousness
The Saintly Level of Consciousness
The Spiritual Level of Consciousness
The Human Level of Consciousness
The Animalistic Level of Consciousness

There's an eighth level of consciousness also. There are even infinite higher levels than the godly level of consciousness. In the godly level of consciousness, a human being cares for other human beings more than he cares for his own little self. And, the godly human being lives to make other human beings happy.

In the eighth level of consciousness, a human being isn't anything other than, at the most decent level, doing the Will of the Creator. There aren't too many human beings that attain the eighth level of consciousness in this material level of coming into the worlds of the Creator. This little world is the first coming into being of all little human beings, who even all start off at the atom level of consciousness. Most two-legged human beings leave this plane of existence even at the human level of consciousness. Only a few venture into the spiritual level of consciousness and above.

There's a saying of Krishna, with God speaking through Krishna, that even says this:

Out of a thousand souls,
Only one seeks Me.
Out of a thousand souls that seek Me,
Only one finds Me.
Out of a thousand souls that find Me,
Only one knows Me.

In the real Jacob's Ladder, there are nine levels of initial consciousness of little human beings. There are three levels of Jacob's Ladder that are below the two-legged so called human level. When the little human beings come into Existence, they come into the mineral kingdom and progress up to the little plant kingdom and then to the little so called animal kingdom. When the Creator knows that a little human being is ready for the little two-legged so called human being little station, He causes any little human being so called animal to even be born into the so called human kingdom of Existence. When the little human being is born into the little so called human kingdom of Existence, he or she only has the animalistic qualities and attributes and virtues that it acquired as a little so called animal. That little animalistic human being learns how to even be a so called human being. That little human being is born very ignorant and needs to learn even everything that he or she can in order to be happy and progress in the little material existence that he or she has even been born into. When that little human being needs a little help, the Creator assists him or her into even becoming a little spiritual so called human being. Little human beings that seek out their Creator aren't nothing other than assisted to even progress up Jacob's little ladder even as far up as they even have the incentive and determination to climb Jacob's little ladder in their little lifetime. Little human beings that are very, very seeking out their Creator even end up literally hundreds of thousands of little levels above the little animalistic level of consciousness. Little human beings who seek out their Creator most all of the little time aren't anything other than greatly assisted by their Creator to climb Jacob's little ladder even to the little limit of Jacob's little ladder, where further climbing is limited to the next little existence. The little human beings that climb Jacob's little ladder all the way to the little top of it, aren't anything other than having entered a realm of Existence that is sanctified from little human conditions and even a godly realm of Existence that has even a little million levels of consciousness that are even incorporated into the little souls of the inhabitants of the godly realm of Existence. When a little ignorant human being is assisted by his or her Creator to even enter this realm of Existence, the little human being starts to lose his or her little ignorance and is even then learning who he or she really is, and, when the little ignorant human being learns about who he or she is, he or she starts entering the infinite realm of Existence and then even knows who he or she is and even then given a new little name that signifies the little station of the now infinite little human being that is even now a little preparing for his or her little creatorhood little station. When the little new infinite little human being learns his little lessons, he or she

43

enters a new realm of Existence that is called the little station of godhood. When the little godhood little human being learns his or her little lessons, he or she enters the domain of little Poverty in human qualities and human attributes and human virtues, and grows and develops and matures and evolves in godly qualities and godly attributes and godly virtues that are vastly different from the little human being godly qualities and the little human being godly attributes and the little human being godly virtues. That little human being isn't anything other than now really being prepared for his or her little creatorhood little station. When the little human being even becomes a little creator, he or she isn't really any little human being any longer, but a little thing of things that isn't quite able to be described in little human vocabulary. That little thing of things surrounds the infinite surroundings of little Infinity. The little thing of things surrounds even more than Infinity. That little thing of things isn't anything other than capable of, when he or she is fully developed and matured and evolved as a little thing of things, capable of many little supernatural little things!!!

Jacob's Ladder in the infinite realm isn't nothing other than very different from the other little realms. When a little godly realm human being gets to the infinite realm, he or she becomes a little knowledgeable about Existence. When that little infinite realm human being even thinks about anything, little thoughts will pop into his or her little consciousness that'll even elucidate on the thing or things thought about. That little realm isn't any small little realm at all, howbeit, in the infinite realm, little infinite realm human beings thoughtfully challenge the Creator to even divulge even everything about Existence to the little infinite realm little human being. The little infinite realm human being even kind of absorbs infinite knowledge and even when thinking about any little subject, the little thoughts will pop into his or her consciousness that'll clarify the little subject thought about. When the little infinite realm human being gets through with knowing every little thing that even exists, he or she will even be almost ready for the little thing of things little station. We'll even elucidate on the little thing of things little station. When the little thing of things little station happens to envelop the little infinite realm little human being, nothing other than saying, the little infinite realm little human being will even be a little powerful in his or her little consciousness, and, even emit many little vibrations that'll even cause other little ignorant human beings to even grow and develop and mature and evolve at a rapidly greater rate of growing and developing and maturing and evolving than they are presently moving at. When that little human being doesn't like offering up his or her little life and his or her little soul and his or her little being and his or her little qualities and his or her little attributes and his or her little virtues and his or her little everything for the sake of his or her little fellow human beings, the Creator will even cause that little human being to even stay at that little level of the infinite realm human being until they are ready to even offer up their little ignorant everything for the sake of their fellow human beings. That little infinite realm little human being isn't any little thing, howbeit, without any little doubt, with the offering up of the little everything for the sake of human beings, that little infinite realm human being will even grow and develop and mature and evolve even at a phenomenal rate of growing and developing and maturing and evolving to even attain that little thing of things little station. When that little ignorant human being, at any little time, offers up his or her little everything for the sake of human beings, their little progress up Jacob's little ladder will increase even at a phenomenal little rate of ascending all the way to the little thing of things little station. When the little ignorant human being offers up the little everything for the sake of human beings, the little soul causes the little human being to even acquire a little metaphysical little form that'll even never be sick or even deteriorate too much until the little Angel Gabriel, the Angel of Death, takes them away.

THE REALMS OF EXISTENCE: There are nine Realms of Existence. Nothing other than saying, the first Realm is the Human Realm of Existence. Every human being starts off in Existence in the Human Realm of Existence. The Human Realm of Existence has nine levels. The levels of the Human Realm even have the first little level as the Evil Level of the Human Realm of Existence. The second level is the Animalistic Level. The third level is the Human Level. The fourth level is the Spiritual Level. The fifth level is the Saintly Level, and the sixth level is the Angelic Level, and the seventh level is the Divine Level, and the eighth level is the Godly Level of the Human Realm of Existence. The ninth level of the Human Realm of Existence is the level of being a real human being. In the Human Realm of Existence, a human being is an evil human being or an animalistic human being or a human being or a spiritual human being or a saintly human being or an angelic human being or a divine human being or a godly human

47

being and finally a real human being in the ninth level of the Human Realm of Existence. A little animalistic human being can even linger in the animalistic level or even enter the evil level of the Human Realm of Existence. Once an animalistic human being becomes a human being, he'll never enter the evil level of the Human Realm of Existence.

The second Realm of Existence is the Spiritual Realm of Existence. When a godly human being becomes a real human being, he'll even eventually enter the Spiritual Realm of Existence where he'll even be a spiritual being and not any spiritual human being. There are infinite levels of the Spiritual Realm of Existence. When the Creator deems it right at the appropriate little time, the spiritual being will enter the Saintly Realm of Existence. Then the Angelic Realm. Then the Divine Realm. Then the Godly Realm. All the Realms entered at the bidding of the Creator. The seventh Realm of Existence is the Supreme Being Realm of Existence, where a Godly being becomes a supreme being. The eighth Realm of Existence is the God of Existence Realm of Existence, where a supreme being becomes a god of Existence. And finally the ninth Realm of Existence is the Creatorhood Realm of Existence, where a god of Existence becomes a creator under the supervision of the

Creator, the God of Existence. All of the Realms of Existence, other than the Human Realm, have infinite levels.

All along the little stepping stones up to the Creatorhood Realm of Existence, the ascender is learning even everything about Existence and finally at the Creatorhood Realm of Existence, he'll know even everything about Existence.

All along the way up this ladder of progress, free will can even hinder or help the little ascender up the little ladder of progress. Little by little, eventually every little human being will traverse all of the Realms of Existence, even their Creator assisting even every little human being to attain his or her final destiny of becoming a creator of their own little future selves under the Rulership of the Uncreated Creator of Existence.

Chapter 13
The Future
Monotheistic Religion

The future monotheistic religion won't even be any organized religion at all. It'll be an individual connection between each human being with his Creator. When the small minded adherents of religion think that organized religion is the answer, they're a little misguided. None of the Prophets brought any organized religion to humanity. The real religion is belief in the One True God and following His guidelines for living a decent life. The Ten Commandments of the Mosaic Dispensation aren't anything other than very decent guidelines for living a decent life. The Sermon of the Mount of Jesus the Christ are even a decent little guideline for living a decent life. The spiritual guidelines of even every religion are decent guidelines for living a decent life. There is no need of organized religion for even guiding the human beings into living a decent little life. Human beings can read the Sermon on the Mount for their own selves and read the Scriptures of all the revealed religions for the purpose of finding out what a decent human being does to live a decent little life. There is no need of any paid clergy who only read the Scriptures with their own interpretation which might even be a different interpretation from what a so called lay person might interpret the same Scriptures. The clergy is steeped in traditional interpretation of Scripture and even many are close minded to a different interpretation than their time honored traditional interpretations. Little do you know it, howbeit, the traditional interpretation of the Christian belief system even contradicts the Old Testament Prophets' belief that there is only One God that goes by several different names. The Christian belief traditionally states that there are three persons in one god, all equal to each other. The Old Testament God has no equal. Even the New Testament God isn't anything other than the One True God, howbeit, Christian interpretation is what is making God into three persons, all equal to each other. The God of Islam is the One True God in the Station of Allah. The Hindu God is the One True God in the Station of the Supreme Personality of the Godhead. The Zoroastrian God is the One True God in the Station of Ahura Mazda.

When the little human being begins to seek out his or her Creator in even everything, then the little human being will even seek out his or her Creator in the little consciousness and even start communicating with his or her Creator.

When the little human being seeks out his or her Creator, then the Creator even opens up the little door to His Presence. Nothing other than saying, "Knock, and the door shall be opened unto you."

Chapter 14
Why any Religion at all

Without religion's guidelines, the human beings wouldn't even be as decent as the little so called animals!!! Societies mostly are based on the Ten Commandments' guiding principles. And when a human being is obedient to his government, he's generally a decent human being and living according to his Creator's guidelines for living a decent little life. When religion is an individual thing and not organized, the human beings will even be more open minded for even accepting future decent plans for the furtherance of human knowledge and understanding about many things that are even controversial today because of the close mindedness of many religious human beings. In the future society of open minded human beings, there'll even be a future renaissance of many flavors, no doubt whatsoever.

When the human being seeks his or her God of Existence even in every little thing, the God of Existence will even open the door of His Kingdom which is nothing other than His Presence in the consciousness of the little human being. Nothing other than saying, "Seek, and ye shall find."

Chapter 15
Why aren't the Religions Open Minded

The religions aren't anything other than steeped in tradition and dogma that stems back to the founding of the religions. When the religions aren't steeped in tradition and dogma, then the purport of their Scriptures will even be a little clearer to the reader of their Scripture. For instance, the Catholic religion has an interpretation of the Godhead being three persons in one god. When you try explaining the Gospels in a different interpretation, most Catholics would just ignore your interpretation and maintain their little close mindedness. The Islamic religion believes that Muhammad is the last Prophet based on their interpretation of the Holy Quran. If you try explaining to them the meaning of their Scripture with a different interpretation, they also would ignore your interpretation and maintain their little close mindedness also. Some religions limit God by saying He can't send a Prophet after so and so, or, He can't send a Prophet for a thousand little years, and if you tell them your interpretation of their Scriptures, they'll ignore your interpretation and maintain their little close mindedness also. All of the religions have their little idiosyncrasies that close their little minds to even the expansion of their little minds and further expanding their knowledge and understanding of their own religion. Little close minded adherents of religion aren't anything other than personality worshippers who worship certain personalities that even cause the little adherents of religion to blindly follow the little misguided understanding of the personalities that they even worship. Why do the religious adherents worship personalities??? It's because certain personalities are in little positions of power in the religions and the little parroting adherents think that they're the little authority on even anything concerning that religion. Little parroting religious people parrot their leaders without investigating the truth for their own little selves.

Chapter 16
What is the Destiny
of Human Beings

The little human beings aren't anything other than destined to even be very superhuman human beings. When the little human beings acquire the requisite amount of virtue and spiritual attributes and spiritual qualities, the God of Existence will eventually cause their little human consciousness and their little human form to even be transformed into a higher consciousness and a higher form. When the little human beings even become very altruistic, the God of Existence will even transform them into spiritual giants, even giving them the station of a god of the Supreme Being, nothing other than saying, very altruistic human beings are even destined for what human vocabulary is even incapable of describing. Once the altruistic little human beings decide to offer up their little soul and their little life and their little being and their little qualities and their little attributes and their little virtues and their little everything for the sake of their fellow human beings, the Creator will transform their little soul into a god-soul that'll even cause the offerer up to eventually be a creator of his own little self under the aegis and supervision of the God of Existence, their Creator.

Chapter 17
Suffering Human Beings

When a human being offers to suffer for the sake of his fellow human beings, for the reason of it being, to elevate human beings at the expense of his suffering for them, then the God of Existence will even cause the sufferer for human beings to even be eventually a god of Existence. Don't even think that's the God of Existence, Who is the Creator. The god of Existence station is a little station under the God of Existence. When the offerer up decides to suffer for the sake of advancing the progress of his fellow human beings, then the Creator will even make him a god of Existence, which is the next step upward to even becoming a creator under the authority of his Creator. When the little human being offers up his little everything for the sake of his fellow human beings, every little station available to human beings will even be eventually attained by the offerer up of the little everything. And, the offering up can even be done by an evil little human being and even cause the evil little human being to ascend the ladder of progress, even as a decent human being, even to every little station destined for little human beings.

Chapter 18
The Higher Stations of Human Beings

The higher stations of human beings aren't nothing other than stations of self-control and self-sacrifice. The higher stations are attained by the little human being exhibiting extreme self-control and extreme self-sacrifice. When a little human being controls his little self even from doing evil and ignorant little things, that little human being has even controlled the little animal personality within the soul of even every little human being. Little human beings who even offer to sacrifice their little everything for the sake of their fellow human beings, will even eventually attain the highest stations available to the human being. When a human being offers up his little soul and his little life and his little being and his little virtues and his little qualities and his little attributes and his little everything for the sake of his fellow human beings, the God of Existence will even anoint that little human being with a little beginning station of god of the Supreme Being, which is the station of doing the Will of the God of Existence to even a superlative degree. When a little god of the Supreme Being offers to suffer for the sake of helping his fellow human beings, the God of Existence will even anoint that little human being with a station of even being a god of Existence under the God of Existence. That last station is even living according to the Will of the Creator at even a highest degree, even higher than a superlative degree. Little human beings who are altruistic, are even the highest human beings, in character.

Chapter 19
The One True God

The One True God is Infinite in all respects. He has no limitations, not even bound by His Scriptures. He doeth whatsoever He Willeth. The One True God isn't any little thing that some little human beings even believe that He is. Nothing other than saying, the One True God can do anything any little human being can even conceive of. He can even do anything He can conceive of, and, no little human being can even conceive of what the One True God can conceive of. The One True God is so Infinitely Infinite that He Surrounds Infinite Space and even Surrounds the surrounding of Infinite Space, even Surrounding any surrounding of Infinite Space, even infinite surroundings of Infinite Space. Each surrounding of Infinite Space is more infinite than the previous surrounding of Infinite Space!!! He is even Infinite in every Attribute and every Virtue and every Quality. Even little human language is inadequate to define or describe any Quality or Attribute or Virtue of the One True God!!! The human qualities and attributes and virtues only inadequately describe the Qualities and the Attributes and the Virtues of the Creator. The little human languages can't even give an adequate name to the so called Creator. One True God isn't really defining or describing the Creator!!! What human being can even define the Word "God." Or, what human being can even define "Creator" as it pertains to the Ultimate Reality. That Ultimate Reality will never ever be completely known or understood by even any little human being. The finite cannot surround the Infinite. And, in order to know or understand the Infinite, you need to surround the Infinite!!! What kind of Creator is so Big that the little finite human being doesn't even exist compared to the Creator??? Well that's how it is!!!

The God of Existence Station isn't anything other than His Ruling Station over His Existences. The God of Existence isn't anything other than the God that created Existence. Nothing other than saying, the God of Existence Station is one of His infinite Stations. And, even within the God of Existence Station, there are even infinite Stations. Nothing other than saying, the Father Station, the Allah Station, the Yahweh Station, the Jehovah Station, the Elohim Station and the Ahura Mazda Station are all some of His infinite Stations as a God. Other Stations are the Buddha Station and the Krishna Station that are known. The little ignorant human beings aren't anything other than ignorant and non-existent compared to the God of Existence. When the little human beings offer up their little soul and their little life and their little being and their little qualities and their little attributes and their little virtues and their little everything for the sake of their fellow human beings, then and only then will the Creator start revealing more of Himself to the little ignorant human beings.

Chapter 20
The Goal of Existence

Nothing other than saying, the goal of Existence is for the inhabitants of Existence to attain even every station destined for little ignorant human beings. Little ignorant human beings aren't anything other than needing to rid their little selves of their profound ignorance of their purpose for being in the existences of the Existences of the **EXISTENCE** of the God of Existence. Little ignorant human beings who live for material pleasures and material pursuits aren't anything other than out of touch with the purpose for which they were even created!!! Little ignorant human beings who ignore the prophets or the messengers or the gurus of their Creator and pursue material concerns only aren't even anything other than hindering their own progress up the little ladder of progress and are out of touch with the purpose for which they were even created. This little chapter doesn't even be what we're wanting it to be, meaning nothing other than, this little chapter isn't anything other than kind of chastening the little ignorant human beings that are stagnating spiritually in this world, for the reason of not wanting to be religiously active or correcting their gross and even evil behavior, and pursuing material pursuits only without growing and developing and maturing and evolving spiritually. What kind of Creator would allow any complacent little human being into His heaven or His paradise??? What kind of Creator would even allow any suicide bomber into His heaven or His paradise??? What kind of Creator would even allow any evil human being into His heaven or His paradise??? And what kind of human being, who is complacent or evil or physically maturing at the expense of growing spiritually, would even think that God would allow him or her into His heaven or His paradise??? Nothing other than saying, the Creator doesn't like these kinds of little ignorant human beings, howbeit he allows them into His heaven or paradise after their demise, howbeit, not without a little Chastening and Counseling after their little death, and, under the condition of them working hard to correct their little selves in their little ignorant little beliefs and their little ignorant little behaviors while in the heaven or paradise of the God of Existence.

Chapter 21
How do you Grow Spiritually

Many little ignorant human beings aren't anything other than very prejudiced against some little thing, some little belief, or some little group of human beings or even one little human being or a host of other little things. The little prejudiced human being needs to examine his reasons for his prejudice and even study what he's prejudiced against or immerse himself in a group of people that he's prejudiced against. Some little human beings are very self-centered and need to even volunteer helping those in need. Some human beings are even very irresponsible and need to even just correct that little evil behavior with a determined conscious effort. There are many little human beings who procrastinate and they even need to make conscious effort to not put off 'til tomorrow what can even be done today. Some human beings are very very irresponsible and need some professional counseling to even correct their very evil behavior. Little evil human beings don't even like correcting their little evil behavior. Howbeit, this little chapter is even giving them a little alternative, which is, continue your irresponsible little evil behavior and, at your little demise, welcome a little chastening and counseling from the God of Existence. When the little cock crows, little dawn is coming, and, this little book signals the dawn of a new little creation where the spiritually deprived will even suffer for their spiritual deprivation!!!

Growing spiritually happens even when a person attempts to do his or her best at whatever he or she is doing. Strive for perfection!!!

Chapter 22
What kind of Existence
is This???

This Existence doesn't even be the only Existence of the God of Existence. There are even many infinite numbers of Existences. There aren't nothing other than Existences that are very different from this little Universe. This little Existence that I call a Universe doesn't even be anything other than the first little Universe in which little two-legged little so called human beings have been brought into Existence. When the God of Existence creates a little human being, He isn't even unaware that the little human being is a little inherently evil and, considering this, the God of Existence causes His Self to Appear as His Prophets for the education of the little ignorant human beings. When the little human beings accept the Prophets of the God of Existence, they are even forgiven all of their past transgressions and even are advised to sin no more, as Jesus the Christ told a little sinner who accepted His Prophethood, nothing other than, "Go, and sin no more."

The little ignorant human beings that even are satisfied with their little condition are a little complacent and need to work on growing and maturing and evolving spiritually to a higher level of spirituality than their present level of spirituality. The little human beings who work toward ascending the little ladder of progress will even be happier and even be progressing for even all eternity to even be more and more and more in the image and the likeness of their God of Existence.

Chapter 23
The gods of the Creator

A little spiritual human being doesn't even be anything other than decently decent as a little human being! When a spiritual human being enters the godly level of the Human Realm of Existence, the God of Existence will even start the process of causing that little human being to even be a god of the Supreme Being. A god of the Supreme Being doesn't even be anything other than intellectually genius and even emotionally mature. There are many levels of the God of the Supreme Being little station. The little god of Existence station is even attained after the little god of the Supreme Being station has been attained.!

Chapter 24
The Human Being

When a little so called human being enters the godly level of Existence, he starts to even become a real human being. There aren't any real human beings on this little planet. The little human beings that enter the godly level of Existence aren't anything other than starting to even become a real human being, nothing other than saying, little selfish and ignorantly immature human beings aren't any real human beings, let alone, evil human beings. Little evil human beings even are less than the little so called animals. Animalistic human beings are even on a little level with the little animals. Selfish human beings aren't even that human. When little selfish human beings start becoming a little altruistic, their progress up the ladder of progress even increases dramatically. Little materialistic human beings who live for physical pleasures and enjoyment aren't anything other than very animalistic and not even human beings.

Chapter 25
The Eight Kinds of Love

AGAPE LOVE—This is the Love of the Creator for His Own Self.

Out of Agape Love springs forth Love for the Creation and everything in the Creation.

The next love is the love of human beings for the Creator. It springeth out of faith in there being a Higher Power. Loving the Creator is even causing four other loves to come into being.
1. Love of a human being for another human being.
2. Love of a human being for the Creation.
3. Love of a human being for all other human beings that even exist.
4. Love of a human being for his own little self.

The eighth love is the little sexual attraction of one human being for another human being. This is a physical love.

The love of an atheist isn't any love at all but a selfish little kind of so called love.

The little love of a child for its parents is also a selfish little kind of so called love until a divine love is established in the child.

When you're attracted to someone sort of mentally or emotionally, it's the human love or what is called spiritual love.

The Divine Love is the Love of the Prophet for the little human beings that seek out their Creator. The little Divine Love is even a ninth kind of Love. It's even within the Love of the Creator for His Creation.

There are even many other little loves that are offshoots of the nine kinds of love. For instance, love of a human being for even any little thing isn't anything other than stemming from the love of the Creation.

The little love of animals for each other isn't nothing other than the love of a human being for another human being.

The little love of an atom for another atom isn't anything other than called chemical bonding or nothing other than electrically opposite charges attracting each other.

Nothing other than saying, gravity is the love of a celestial body for the things that are upon it.

Nothing other than saying, the planets revolve around the sun because the love of the sun for the planets keeps them close to a certain degree.

Little fish aren't anything other than attracted to each other, other than the predator species, because of the love of a human being for another human being.

Stars circle around a central star that is even the prophet star because of their love for the prophet star.

Little ants aren't anything other than little human beings that love their queen.

Little bees also love their queen bee.

Flies aren't even not loving little two-legged human beings. That's why they're always around little two-legged human beings.

The moon loves the little earth and kind of revolves around the little earth for showing its love for the little earth.

All of the galaxies move around this little galaxy that we all live in because this galaxy is the dawning place of the Prophets of the Supreme God of Existence.

Chapter 26
Agape Love

When the Creator Loves His Own Self, He even Loves His Creation, for His Qualities and His Attributes and His Virtues necessitate Him having a Creation. Without a Creation the Creator wouldn't even be fulfilling His Potential that is even directed by His Qualities and His Attributes and His Virtues.

The Creator Loves His creatures even as much as He Loves His Own little Self, for His Love isn't divided into parts that are different for His Own Self and different for His creatures.

Little ignorant human beings need to love their Creator also, for the Love of the Creator cannot even affect the creatures unless they love the Creator also. Little ignorant human beings little love isn't as powerful as the Love of the Creator. Little ignorant human beings need to love even every other little human being and eventually need to love the entire Creation.

The little creatures aren't anything other than created out of Love. The little creatures aren't anything other than needing to even love each other more than words can possibly convey. The little love of the creatures for each other will even cause civilization to blossom into eventually the Kingdom of the God of Existence.

When the Kingdom of the God of Existence comes into being, nothing can undermine the civilization of the Kingdom of the God of Existence. Little ignorant human beings that love material things will surely be surprised, for the next Existence isn't that material, and the little ignorant human beings need to even be a little detached from material things in order to prosper in the next Existence, nothing other than saying, period.

Chapter 27
Agape Love in the Prophets

The Prophets are the Creator Manifesting through a little ignorant human being, who is the little prophet with a small "p." When the Prophets Manifest Themselves, They are the Supreme God of Existence Manifesting in various little Stations. The little Stations are little because they aren't what the Supreme God of Existence really is. Some of the little Stations aren't nothing other than, the Father little Station, the Elohim little Station, the Yahweh little Station, the Jehovah little Station, the Allah little Station and even the Supreme Personality of the Godhead little Station. When the Stations are Revealed, they are even the Stations of what a little ignorant human being can even kind of comprehend. When the Supreme God of Existence Manifests His Self as the Father, He isn't anything other than saying that He Watches over His little ignorant little human beings. And, nothing other than saying, when He Manifests His Self as Allah, He is even saying that He is the Creator of little human beings and even rewards decent human beings and even chastens evil human beings. When the Supreme God of Existence Manifests His Self as Elohim and Yahweh and Jehovah in the Old Testament, He is even saying that He goes by many different little names. When He Manifests His Self as the Supreme Personality of the Godhead, He is even saying that He is the God of Existence, Who is even the Supreme Personality of the Godhead, His little Self Only.

When the God of Existence Manifests His little Self, He Manifests even so little because little ignorant human beings can't even comprehend the little bit that He Manifests. When little human beings figure out what the God of Existence really is, they'll even leap for joy at such a revelation of Glory and Power and a little everything conceivable in the God of Existence. Little ignorant human beings don't even understand exactly what a God is, let alone the Supreme God of Existence. When little ignorant human beings learn what the God of Existence is capable of doing, they'll even be so dumbfounded, they'll even be in a little stupor for even forevermore.

Chapter 28
Backbiting

Backbiting is telling a lie or a truth about a little human being that hurts his or her character. If something said about someone causes others to dislike or hate that person, then it's backbiting. Backbiting is a serious little sin that is prohibited by the God of Existence.

Chapter 29
Little gods of Existence

When little human beings become spiritual, they'll even at some little point, be given a little station of a "god of Existence." That little "god" is with a small little "g", meaning a little human being little god. A little human being little god isn't nothing other than a superior little human being in intellect and emotions and various other little qualities and attributes and virtues.

When the little god of Existence nothing other than decides to offer up his or her little soul and his or her little life and his or her little being and his or her little qualities and his or her little attributes and his or her little virtues and his or her little everything for the sake of human beings, then the Creator will even greatly assist those little human beings in climbing the little ladder of progress. Any little human being can even offer up their little everything for the sake of human beings and even be assisted to even attain that little "god of Existence" little station and even further attain the other stations ordained for little ignorant human beings to even be attaining.

Chapter 30
Offering Up Little Station

When a little ignorant human being offers up his little soul and his little life and his little being and his little qualities and his little virtues and his little attributes and his little everything for the sake of human beings, the Creator will even know if it's done a little altruistically or not, and if it's not done altruistically, it won't even be accepted by the God of Existence.

Chapter 31
He is all of the Prophets

Little ignorant human beings aren't even aware that the real Prophet with a capital "P" isn't anything other than the Supreme God of Existence. Little ignorant human beings don't even be understanding that God speaks through the chosen prophet with a small "p." The real Prophet, the God of Existence, has All Knowledge and All Power and He doeth all of the miracles that are done in certain dispensations. When the real Prophet speaks, the little human being prophet just listens in his little consciousness and even is one of the recipients of the Revelation of the Supreme God of Existence, in even any of His little Stations. In the Islamic religion the Holy Quran was Revealed by the real Prophet, God His Own little Self. Literally speaking, God is the first Prophet and the last Prophet and even all of the little Prophets, nothing other than saying, the Supreme God of Existence isn't anything other than, even in any dispensation, the first little Prophet and the last little Prophet. Nothing other than saying, Muhammad even said, "I am all of the Prophets." That Muhammad wasn't anything other than the

God of Existence speaking through the little human being prophet, Muhammad.

Chapter 32
A Prophet Appears When God Deems it Appropriate

When the little ignorant human beings limit their Creator by saying that He can't do this or He can't do that, they're in grievous error. Some little ignorant human beings limit their Creator by saying that He can't send a Prophet after Moses or He can't send a Prophet after Jesus or He can't send a Prophet after Muhammad, and some little ignorant human beings are even saying God can't send a Prophet for a full thousand little years. Even one of these little ignorant little religions even says about the Creator that, "He doeth whatsoever He Willeth." Yet they persist in their spurious interpretation of their Scripture and insist that the Creator won't send a Prophet for a full thousand little years. Even in the Jewish religion there is a spurious little belief that their Creator won't send a Prophet after Moses. How can little ignorant human beings put limitations on the Creator of this infinite Universe???

Chapter 33
God isn't a Human Being

Although God can appear as a little human being, that human being isn't the Reality of what the God of Existence really is. Little ignorant human beings aren't anything other than confusing the Real Speaker, the God of Existence, with the little ignorant human being form that the God of Existence uses to convey His Message to the little ignorant human beings.

Chapter 34
What Race is my prophet

When the little prophet of the real Prophet comes among little ignorant human beings, he isn't any special race, nothing other than saying, race isn't any determinant of whose prophet the prophet is. What it meaneth isn't nothing other than, a Jewish prophet or a Negro prophet or an Asian prophet is for all of the little ignorant human beings. God doesn't Cause His little prophets to be accepted based on their race. It's a little fact that some little ignorant human beings expect a prophet of their race to even be manifested. Howbeit, the Creator is the real Prophet through the chosen human being prophet. Little ignorant human beings aren't even excused for rejecting any prophet based on his or her little racial orientation. When little ignorant human beings reject the little human being prophets of the real Prophet, the God of Existence, they even deprive themselves of the flowing Grace and Bounty coming forth from the God of Existence. Why doesn't a human being realize that all of the so called races have had prophets among their little civilizations. There have been Asian prophets and there have been Negro prophets and there have been Caucasian prophets and even many Jewish prophets. And, they are coming for the benefit of all little ignorant human beings. Little ignorant Jewish prophets have even been the prophets of the Old Testament and even the Jewish Messiah wasn't anything other than clothed in a Jewish little ignorant human being little form, meaning the God of Existence Spoke through Jesus the Nazarene, a Jewish little prophet. And, nothing other than saying, Lao Tse wasn't anything other than a little Asian prophet whose sayings evolved from the God of Existence Speaking through little Lao Tse. Even the little Confucius wasn't anything other than a little Asian prophet who the God of Existence even Spoke through also. There have been American Indian prophets and Indian prophets, all pertinent to any little ignorant human being. Little ignorant human beings don't like submitting their little ignorant little selves under some little prophet that is of a different little racial orientation from their little racial orientation. The Messengers of the God of Existence aren't anything other than little prophets also and are of all racial orientations. And, all of them are pertinent to even every little ignorant little human being.

Chapter 35
Scriptural Interpretation

Little ignorant human beings interpret Scripture a little erroneously for the most little part. Little ignorant human beings aren't even capable of interpreting Scripture without the help of the real Prophet, the God of Existence, helping them to understand the real meaning of the Scriptures. When the real Prophet is in the world, the little human beings should even ask Him what certain Scriptures even be meaning. Nothing other than saying, the little ignorant human beings aren't the author of the Scriptures and shouldn't even think that they know the meaning of the Scriptures. Only the Author of Scripture Knows the meaning of His Scriptures.

Chapter 36
Human Beings are Complacent

Little human beings are a little self-satisfied with their condition and don't like growing and maturing and developing and evolving into a more mature and more developed little human being. Little ignorant human beings, for the most part, are satisfied with their character and their little emotions and avoid the situations where their character could even be improved or their emotions a little more developed.

Chapter 37
Human Beings aren't Wanting to Seek out their Creator

When the little Prophets appear, the little ignorant human beings don't even investigate their claims. The little ignorant human beings aren't even liking seeking out their Creator for the little reason of it being, seeking human beings are even labeled religious fanatics. The little seeking human beings aren't anything other than controlled by the little ignorant opinions of their little ignorant little associates and even be losing their little souls for even fearing the little judgment of their little ignorant little peers.

When the little ignorant human being decides to seek out his Creator, the Creator Will even map out a little path for the little seeker to follow, even Guiding the little seeker all along that little path to His final destination, His Creator.

Chapter 38
Seeking isn't even Conducive to Anything Other than Destiny Fulfillment

Why do the Prophets come to this little earthen little existence??? The Prophets, meaning the God of Existence, Appears in the form of one of His little ignorant human beings for the purpose of enlightening the little ignorant human beings with His Word, Which is the Water of life to the little withered souls that He even Comes to at the time when their little souls are arid and missing the Water of life. Little ignorant human beings need the Word of the God of Existence for even causing their little souls to blossom and bloom without any little weeds of prejudice of any kind or any thorns of hatred for any other human being or any dry and withered little bushes that are dry and withered lacking the Water of life. The little ignorant human beings who seek out their Creator aren't any little ignorant human beings. Little ignorant evil human beings that seek out their Creator will even be assisted to find their Creator even within their little consciousnesses. When the little ignorant human beings seek out their Creator, they are even fulfilling their little destiny.

Chapter 39
What does Rejection
of the Prophets Cause
in Little Human Beings

The rejection of the Prophets causes the little ignorant human beings to stagnate in one little condition. When the little ignorant human beings reject the Prophets and, or the Messengers and, or the other Sent little Beings, they tamper with their own little souls. What it meaneth isn't nothing other than, the tampering is even like not watering a little flower bush. The Prophets aren't anything other than bringing little things that are even Water to the little souls. When the little ignorant little human being rejects the Watering of his little soul, he even commits spiritual suicide.

Chapter 40
The Father Station

In the Father Station of the God of Existence, the Creator is even Telling little ignorant human beings nothing other than, God created little ignorant human beings and even Watches over them for their decency or their evilness. The Creator, in His Father Station, doesn't even be the Stern Lord of the Old Testament or the Stern Lord of His Allah Station. When little ignorant human beings disobey the Father of little ignorant human beings, the Father Chastens them with various little chastenings. When little ignorant human beings are decent in obeying the Father, the Father even Gives them a little Blessing.

Chapter 41
The Allah Station

When the God of Existence is in His Allah little Station, He even Chastens His creatures for disobeying Allah. When the little human beings are decent in the Islamic religion, Allah even Grants them a little Blessing. When little ignorant human beings enter the Islamic religion, the God of Existence forgives them of all of their little sins. Same thing for any little religion. Little human beings that reflect on the Scriptures aren't anything other than going to even be Guided by the God of Existence into even understanding the Scriptures.

Chapter 42
The Elohim Station

In the Elohim Station of the God of Existence, the God of Existence Chastens little disobedient little Jews who violate the Ten Commandments. And, nothing other than saying, when a Jew is decent, the God of Existence even Grants him or her a little Blessing. Elohim is the Name of the God of Existence that the Jewish people call Him by.

Chapter 43
The Yahweh Station

The God of Existence in His Yahweh Station doesn't anything other than Chasten the Infidels who are the non-believers in the Creator, when the non-believers violate any civil law.

Chapter 44
The Jehovah Station

In the Jehovah Station, the God of Existence even Chastens any little ignorant human being who even violates any civil law.

Chapter 45
The God of Existence Station

In the God of Existence little Station, the God of Existence is Creating a new Existence out of the old Existence. Even in this little Station, the Creator is even taking over all of His little Stations, meaning nothing other than, He is Acting only in the God of Existence little Station. Nothing other than saying, the God of Existence little Station isn't anything other than having all of the other Stations within it. Namely, the Father Station, the Allah little Station, the Elohim little Station, the Yahweh little Station, the Jehovah little Station, even the little Krishna little Station, and even the little Buddha little Station, and even the little Ahura Mazda little Station are all in the God of Existence little Station.

Chapter 46
Parables Clarified

When the parables aren't even understood, they're usually a little allegory. When the parable is even understood, it's usually very misunderstood. When the little parable is an allegory, it's a little esoteric little knowledge that is divulged in the little parable.

Chapter 47
He Who Sits On The Throne

He Who sits on the Throne isn't anything other than the little minor and major prophets of the God of Existence. Little ignorant minor and major prophets aren't anything other than the intermediary chosen little human beings that the God of Existence uses to convey His Message to all of the little ignorant human beings, nothing other than saying, the Real Prophet, the God of Existence, Speaks through the little ignorant minor and the little ignorant major prophets with a little small "p." Now and then the Creator Sits on the Throne His Own little Self. Howbeit, that's another little story that's a little hidden at this little moment.

Chapter 48
The Four Gospels

The four Gospels are even eye witnessed accounts of the Ministry of Jesus the Christ, nothing other than saying, Jesus the Christ is the God of Existence. Little Jesus the human being wasn't Jesus the Christ. All of the statements in the Gospels by Jesus were the statements of the God of Existence through Jesus the human being. The God of Existence took over the little human being form of Jesus the human being when He Spoke to the multitudes. Nothing other than saying, Jesus the Christ isn't nothing other than the little Station of the God of Existence in the little Christian Dispensation.

Chapter 49
The Bible as a Whole

The Bible as a whole isn't nothing other than very allegorical and even needs deep meditation on certain little topics to even be understanding these certain little topics. The Bible isn't even understood in many little Books of the Bible, for many Books of the Bible are interpreted for a different time than this little time. For instance, the Book of Isaiah isn't for this little time, it's for a future little time period, namely thousands of little years in the future.

Chapter 50
The Quran as a Whole

When the Creator Revealed the Holy Quran to the Arabic Peninsula, He even Revealed it through Muhammad, His little ignorant human being little prophet. The Surahs of the Quran aren't even understood for the same little reason as the Books of the little Bible not being understood, other than certain ones that even pertain to this little time period.

Chapter 51
War

War doesn't even be anything other than a little ignorant little thing for decent human beings to even be involved in. Jesus the Christ said, "Blessed are the peacemakers." And, Christians fight against Christians. Even Muslims believe in the prophethood of Jesus and Muslims fight against Muslims and even against Christians and even against Jews. What kind of Christian or what kind of Muslim ignores an admonition of a Prophet that they even believe in???

Chapter 52
Marriage

Marriage, in the New and the Old Testament, wasn't anything other than between a male and a female. Marriage is for sharing life together with the ultimate goal of raising decent little children.

Chapter 53
Civil Law

Little civil law is even from the Creator. When Jesus the Creator Spoke to His disciples, He even told them nothing other than, "Render unto Caesar the things that are Caesar's, and unto God the things that are God's." Caesar was the ruler at that little time and the disciples needed to render obedience to Caesar as well as to Jesus the Creator. If the civil law wasn't from the Creator, Jesus the Creator wouldn't have even given respect to it.

Chapter 54
Divine Law

Divine law comes from God the Creator through His chosen little ignorant human being. When the divine law is Revealed, God Causes even every little ignorant human being to even be under the same divine law.

The Ten Commandments are the Laws of the Old Testament and the New Testament. And, the Sermon on the Mount are decent guidelines for the New Testament. Little other divine laws have even been Revealed and even pertain only to certain people. Little laws for this time period are even contained in Chapter 95 and, sort of, in the Appendix.

Chapter 55
Parable of the Talents

St. Matthew 25:14 through 25:30

For the kingdom of heaven is as a man traveling into a far country, who called his own servants and delivered unto them his goods.

And unto one he gave five talents, to another two, and to another one; to every man according to his several ability; and straightway took his journey.

Then he that had received the five talents went and traded with the same, and made them other five talents.

And likewise he that had received two, he also gained other two.

But he that had received one went and digged in the earth, and hid his lord's money.

After a long time the lord of those servants cometh, and reckoneth with them.

And so he that had received five talents came and brought other five talents, saying, Lord, thou deliveredst unto me five talents: behold, I have gained beside them five talents more.

His lord said unto him, Well done, thou good and faithful servant; thou hast been faithful over a few things, I will make thee ruler over many things: enter thou into the joy of thy lord.

He also that had received two talents came and said, Lord, thou deliveredst unto me two talents: behold, I have gained two other talents beside them.

His lord said unto him, Well done, good and faithful servant; thou hast been faithful over a few things, I will make thee ruler over many things: enter thou into the joy of thy lord.

Then he which had received the one talent came and said, Lord, I knew thee that thou art an hard man, reaping where thou hast not sown, and gathering where thou hast not strawed:

And I was afraid, and went and hid my talent in the earth; lo, there thou hast that is thine.

His lord answered and said unto him, Thou wicked and slothful servant, thou knewest that I reap where I sowed not, and gather where I have not strawed:

Thou oughtest therefore to have put my money to the exchangers, and then at my coming I should have received mine own with usury.

Take therefore the talent from him, and give it unto him which hath ten talents.

For unto every one that hath shall be given, and he shall have abundance: but from him that hath not shall be taken away even that which he hath.

And cast ye the unprofitable servant into outer darkness: there shall be weeping and gnashing of teeth.

This little parable isn't that clear. It doesn't even be meaning anything other than that when a human being is born, he is having certain qualities and attributes and virtues that he even acquired in previous little lives, nothing other than saying, the two decent servants acquired more spiritual qualities and more spiritual attributes and more spiritual virtue in their little lifetime. The unfaithful servant was complacent and self-satisfied and didn't grow and develop and mature and evolve spiritually during his little lifetime and even was cast into outer darkness, which meaneth that he was, at his death, placed in a condition of unconsciousness, kind of, while waiting for his Lord to even speak to him before he entered heaven. His Lord would have even revealed to him what he should have done in his little life and even verbally chastened him and even told him that in heaven, he needed to acquire more spiritual characteristics because he's a little behind the other little human beings.

The weeping and gnashing of teeth isn't anything other than the unfaithful servant's relatives weeping for his little soul at his little funeral.

Chapter 56
Incarnations in the Hindu Religion

The Incarnations in the Hindu religion aren't nothing other than the God of Existence Manifesting His Self in a little ignorant human being little form. When the God of Existence Manifests His little Self in a little human being little form, He is the Incarnation and not the little human being whose form He Manifests His Self in.

Chapter 57
Buddhas in Buddhism

Nothing other than saying, the Buddhas of the Buddhist religion aren't anything other than the God of Existence Manifesting His little Self in a human being little form. The Buddha is the God of Existence and not the little ignorant human being whose form the God of Existence Manifests His little Self in.

Chapter 58
The Little Future of the Religion of the God of Existence

The religion of the God of Existence isn't anything other than a little starting at this little period of little time. Little people who accept the beliefs and the tenets of the Church of the God of Existence in the Appendix of this little book, aren't anything other than a little starting their journey on the path to the God of Existence.

The religion of the God of Existence will even envelop humanity at a little distant future little date.

Chapter 59
Esoteric Knowledge

Esoteric knowledge isn't nothing other than knowledge that the Creator has. And, nothing other than saying, little decent human beings who aspire to meet their Creator will even be given esoteric knowledge, nothing other than saying, only the most decent little human beings will even be granted little esoteric knowledge. The little esoteric knowledge even expands the consciousnesses and even causes the recipient to even grow and develop and mature and evolve at a phenomenal little rate of growing and developing and maturing and evolving.

Chapter 60
Prophethood

Don't even think that there are any little human being little prophets. The Real Prophet is the God of Existence. When little human beings are chosen as the intermediary little human being little form, the God of Existence even gives the little chosen human being a little esoteric knowledge.

Chapter 61
Godhood

There is only one Godhood Station and it's the Station of the Creator. The little godhood station with a small "g" isn't anything other than a little super human little human being who is super human only in little intelligence and little emotions.

Chapter 62
Sainthood

Nothing other than saying, the saints of the Catholic Church are even the little God of Existence working through the little human beings that are even called the little saints. Howbeit, the Real Saint is the God of Existence Who even Manifested His little Self through the various saints of the little Catholic Church. Nothing other than saying, the God of Existence has Guided the little Catholic Church in its canonization of the little saints of the Catholic Church.

Chapter 63
Miracles

Miracles aren't even nothing other than the God of Existence Using His Supreme Power to even Perform a little miracle. When the Red Sea was Parted by the God of Existence, Pharaoh's little men were even drowned when the parting was over with and the waters came back together. Lourdes wasn't nothing other than the God of Existence Appearing as the Virgin Mary. Fatimah was the same little thing. The God of Existence even Caused the Virgin Mary to conceive Jesus the human being by a Power of His Supreme Might. Little ignorant human beings don't even like this little chapter, howbeit, the God of Existence even Raised Jesus the human being from the little deceased condition that he was even in. And, even Lazarus was Raised from the little deceased condition that he was even in by the same Power of the Supreme Might of the God of Existence.

Chapter 64
Execution

Execution isn't any small little thing. Little ignorant human beings, supposedly Christian, cause the murdering of little human beings in the name of society protecting itself.

Chapter 65
Little Murdering
Ignorant Muslims

Little ignorant murdering Muslims call themselves little martyrs. This isn't any martyrdom at all, howbeit, cold blooded murder.

Chapter 66
Divorce

Little ignorant human beings aren't even fit to even marry because they're too immature and undeveloped spiritually, nothing other than saying, little marriage takes a mature human being to enter into. Little ignorant common people of this little age aren't even mature enough to realize that growing spiritually is the prime purpose of living in the Existence of the God of Existence. Little ignorant immature human beings don't even be knowing anything about how to raise little children. When the little cock crows, little ignorant little marriage will even be a permanent little thing, for the reason of it being, the God of Existence is even going to make a law that marriage is a permanent little thing and divorce is even abrogated. When little cock crows, the God of Existence will even make everything in the Gospel of the God of Existence even be fulfilled. Little ignorant little predictors of future societies aren't anything other than deluded by their own lack of faith in their Creator even intervening in little human affairs.

Chapter 67
Alcohol

One of the most dangerous drugs around is ethanol, the alcohol in liquor and wine and beer. When little ignorant human beings start drinking intoxicating beverages, they even become very animalistic in their little ignorant little behavior.

Chapter 68
Little Drugs

When a human being consumes hallucinogenic drugs, the little human being even becomes a little lower than a so called animal. This little drug condition in this little age, is even one of the most important little problems to solve. Little ignorant little human beings aren't anything other than unaware that most of the most vicious little crimes are committed under the influence of illicit drugs.

Chapter 69
Prostitution

When little women start selling their little wares, they even are leeches on little small minded little human beings who would even purchase their little wares.

Chapter 70
Little Criminals

The little criminals who continue criminal behavior even after serving time aren't anything other than very derelict in their responsibility as little human beings in the Existences of the God of Existence.

Chapter 71
Child Molesters

Child molesters are even the most depraved little ignorant human beings that even exist in the Existences of the God of Existence.

Little child molesters shouldn't even be anything other than given a little life imprisonment for the protection of society.

Chapter 72
Imprisonment

Little prisons are for the felony convicted little ignorant human beings and not the misdemeanor convicted little ignorant human beings. When a little ignorant human being serves time for a misdemeanor, his little life is ruined and many little times he starts committing little felonies because his prison record causes him to even be breaking the law rather than suffer joblessness or homelessness because of his criminal record.

Chapter 73
Priesthood

Little priests should even be permitted to marry for the reason of it being, the sexual urge in a celibate person is even stronger than that in a promiscuous person.

Chapter 74
Civil Disobedience

Civil disobedience is disobedience to the God of Existence.

Chapter 75
Rape

Rape isn't that little a crime. It infringes on the dignity of a human being. Little rapists aren't nothing other than needing to even be given counseling on what kind of animal he or she is and then sentenced to a little life imprisonment.

Chapter 76
Fornication

Fornication isn't nothing other than sexual intercourse between two unmarried people. It is even a little distraction from the primary purpose of being in the Existences of the God of Existence. When two little ignorant human beings fornicate, they are even forming a sexual aura between them and even causing their little futures to even be entwined for the most little part. When two people fornicate, they even form a sexual bond that is even hard to break, and, if they ever marry someone else, they'll even always be desiring any old fornication little partner which might even lead to adultery and the breaking up of their little marriage. Little single people aren't even absolved from this little predicament. Little single people aren't anything other than having sexual feelings also, and, they even need to consider marrying also.

Chapter 77
Education

Every human being should be educated as to his or her purpose for being in the Existences of the God of Existence. Nothing other than saying, the purpose for being in the Existences of the God of Existence isn't nothing other than, to grow and develop and mature and evolve in spirituality. It meaneth nothing other than the little human being needs to acquire spiritual virtue and spiritual qualities and spiritual attributes.

Chapter 78
Spiritual Qualities

The little spiritual virtues aren't nothing other than very numerous. The little spiritual attributes are even very numerous, and the spiritual qualities are even very numerous. Some of the spiritual qualities aren't nothing other than decent behavior with a respectful little mouth, meaning no vulgarity in the little speech. Some of the spiritual virtues include courtesy and even respect for other human beings. Little virtues aren't nothing other than decent little productive little thoughts about how you can even help another human being be a little happier than they currently are. And, the decent little attributes aren't anything other than, very numerous and can even be found in all of the Holy Books and that's a little recommendation, "Read the Holy Books to see how a decent human being even behaves."

Chapter 79
Irresponsible Behavior

Irresponsible behavior in the Existences of the God of Existence isn't nothing other than, from this little point onward, a little criminal offense. For instance, driving while under the influence of sleepiness, isn't anything other than irresponsible behavior.

Chapter 80
Homelessness

There shouldn't be any homelessness in the existences of the Existences of the **EXISTENCE** of the God of Existence.

Chapter 81
Gambling

When little ignorant human beings gamble, they're wasting their little precious time.

Chapter 82
Racial Prejudice

Little ignorant human beings were created all one little race. The differences among the so called different races isn't nothing other than due to climate conditions and not because one so called race is superior to another little race.

Chapter 83
Rioting

When little ignorant human beings destroy buildings and loot, they're violating the commandments of the God of Existence. Looting is stealing, and forbidden by the command of the God of Existence in the Ten Commandments. Rioting is also forbidden by the God of Existence in the Bible where Jesus says to "Render unto Caesar the things that are Caesar's, and unto God the things that are God's." Rendering unto Caesar means obeying the civil laws. Rendering unto God meaneth nothing other than obeying the commandments of the God of Existence.

Chapter 84
Prejudice of all Sorts

All prejudices cause the little prejudiced one to even be very narrow minded and even very animalistic some of the times.

Chapter 85
Smoking

Smoking isn't anything other than a dirty filthy little habit.

Chapter 86
Dignity of Human Beings

Human beings were created with their little selves being very dignified little human beings. Anything that is undignified for a human being shouldn't even be done by any human being.

Chapter 87
Hunting

Hunting isn't any humane thing for a dignified human being to even be doing.

Chapter 88
Meat Consumption

Little ignorant human beings, with their current little technology, should even be capable of synthesizing meat products and even abandon the consumption of animal products.

Chapter 89
Dignified Relationships Between Men and Women

Little human beings shouldn't even be familiar with the opposite sex. What it meaneth isn't nothing other than that, a man shouldn't touch any female without her consent and even the woman shouldn't touch a male without his consent.

Nothing other than saying, men and women shouldn't even hug each other, other than married couples. Little ignorant some men like to hug little women because they get a sexual feeling when doing it. Same for some females.

Chapter 90
Pornography

Pornography is a little debasing to little human beings. The human form isn't any little plaything for sexual exploitation. When little men and little women engage in pornographic pictures or movies, they are even debasing themselves even before other human beings.

Chapter 91
Wholesome Foods

All of the little plant foods are wholesome little foods. Little grains and nuts and vegetables and fruits are even the decent little foods. Even little beans without any doubt, are decent little foods. Little any kind of plants that produce edible products are decent for the little human beings to even consume. Study some research papers and see that certain combinations of plant items constitute what is called a complete protein. When a complete protein is consumed, all of the amino acids needed to rebuild the body's proteins are made available to the little body for even rebuilding the little molecules that break down during life's strenuous exercise or just everyday living.

Chapter 92
Stem Cell Research

A little embryo is a living organism and even a little human being depending on what organism we're talking about. Little stem cell research isn't anything other than little murdering research.

Chapter 93
Barbaric Laws

Little barbaric laws that maim a little human being for certain little crimes aren't anything other than the most vile thing in the Sight of the God of Existence.

Chapter 94
A New Existence

The God of Existence isn't anything other than Creating a new Existence out of the old Existence. The God of Existence Station isn't anything other than the newest Station of the God of Existence. In the newest little Existence little ignorant human beings aren't any little things like they were in the old Existence. The little ignorant human beings in the old Existence, weren't anything other than able to even become a little prophet under the various Stations of the Creator. Nothing other than saying, in the Christian religion, in the old Existence, a little ignorant human being could even have become a prophet of the Father. In the Jewish religion, the little ignorant human beings could have even become a prophet of Elohim. In the old Existence, a little ignorant human being of the Islamic religion could have even become a prophet of Allah, and in the Buddhist religion, a little ignorant human being could have become a prophet of Buddha, the Real Buddha, the God of Existence. In the Hindu religion, a little ignorant human being could have even become a prophet of Krishna, the Real Krishna, the God of Existence. In the old Existence, a little ignorant human being of the Parsi religion could have even become a prophet of Ahura Mazda, the God of Existence to the Parsi religion. And, in the Baha'i religion, a little ignorant human being could have even become a prophet of Baha'u'llah, the God of Existence Who Spoke through Mirza Hussein Ali.

In the newest little Existence, a little ignorant human being can even become a prophet of the Supreme God of Existence.

Chapter 95
The Laws and Ordinances of the God of Existence

1. Confess sins only to the God of Existence.
2. Praying is essential to spiritual development.
3. Prostitution is forbidden.
4. Reading Scripture is even commanded.
5. The Ten Commandments are even now in force.
6. Racial prejudice and other prejudices are forbidden.
7. Abortion is forbidden.
8. The clergy of all religions is confirmed.
9. The admonitions and ordinances and precepts and the other guidances for living a decent little life in the Scriptures are all in force.

Appendix
The Church of the God of Existence

Nothing other than saying, the Church of the God of Existence isn't any organized religion. It's a set of beliefs and tenets that the followers of the Church of the God of Existence live their lives by, nothing other than saying, the religions of the past aren't anything other than contaminated by the little spurious interpretations of the leaders of those religions. The false interpretations of the leaders of past religions cause the adherents of those religions to even be very narrow minded and even many are very close minded about certain little beliefs that they even accept as even the absolute truth. Truth is relative and not absolute. The little narrow minded practitioners of certain religions even put limitations on the God of Existence. Some even say that the God of Existence can't send His prophets other than according to their narrow minded little limitations. When the God of Existence is limited in any little thing, it's the little ignorant narrow minded human beings who are limiting Him. The God of Existence doeth whatsoever He Willeth or Chooseth to do, even at any period of time in the present or in the future.

155

The Beliefs of the Church of The God of Existence

One God, Who Has Many Names

One Human Race

The One True God Counsels His Creatures In Inspiration And Many Other Ways

Independent Investigation Of All Things

All Atoms And All Plants And All Animals Are Human Beings

All Human Beings Reflect the Creator

All Human Beings Are The Embodiment Of At Least One Attribute Of The Creator

All Of The Religions Are From The Creator

The God Of Existence Surrounds The Infinite Surroundings Of Infinite Space

The Tenets of the Church of the God of Existence

1. Obedience to the government of the land in which you live.
2. Obedience to the laws of any country visited.
3. Obedience to the authority figures of the land in which you live.
4. Obedience to the admonitions of the Scriptures of the God of Existence.
5. Obedience to Scriptures applicable in the present little day.
6. Scriptures aren't to be taken literally other than the admonitions pertaining to decent human behavior.
7. Literally interpret Scripture only when it accords with science and reason.